Sing with Jazzy

Jazzy's Twelve Days of Christmas

by Sonja McGiboney

Copyright 2021
ISBN-978-1-7333663-6-6

four penguin pals,

three smiling elves,

two tennis balls,

and the biggest bone that I have ever seen!

four penguin pals,

three smiling elves,

two tennis balls,

and the biggest bone that I have ever seen!

six sugar cookies,

FIVE BRAIDED ROPES

four penguin pals,

three smiling elves,

two tennis balls,

and the biggest bone that I have ever seen!

four penguin pals,

three smiling elves,

two tennis balls,

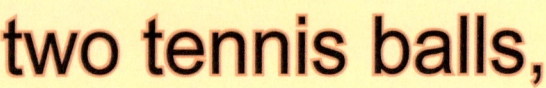
and the biggest bone that I have ever seen!

eight furry friends,

seven sneaky snakes,

six sugar cookies,

FIVE BRAIDED ROPES

four penguin pals,

three smiling elves,

two tennis balls,

and the biggest bone that I have ever seen!

On the tenth day of Christmas, my true love gave to me

ten swimming pigs,

nine pink petunias,

eight furry friends,

seven sneaky snakes,

six sugar cookies,

four penguin pals,

three smiling elves,

two tennis balls,

and the biggest bone that I have ever seen!

seven sneaky snakes,

six sugar cookies,

FIVE BRAIDED ROPES

nine pink petunias,

eight furry friends,

seven sneaky snakes,

six sugar cookies,

three smiling elves,

two tennis balls,

four penguin pals,

FIVE BRAIDED ROPES

and the biggest bone that I have ever seen!

The End

Sonja McGiboney grew up in Stowe, Pennsylvania. After obtaining her undergraduate degree in music from West Virginia University, she married Dale and joined him on his 25-year military career. She has two wonderful children, Rachel and Ryan, and now lives with Dale and Jazzy in Smithfield, Virginia. She loves taking photos and writing Jazzy's Books.

ABC Jazzy
Counting Down Jazzy
Growing Up Jazzy
Jazzy and Friends
Jazzy Colors
Jazzy Time
Jazzy Shapes
Jazzy Explores the Library
Jazzy Explores Smithfield, VA
Jazzy Explores Murfreesboro, NC
Jazzy's Alphabet Adventure (Jan 2022)
Jazzy's Halloween
Jazzy's Twelve Days of Christmas
Little Red Jazzyhood
Princess Jazzy

Subscribe to Jazzy's website and get a free coloring page every month!

https://www.jazzysbooks.com

CPSIA information can be obtained
at www.ICGtesting.com
Printed in the USA
BVRC100025191121
621977BV00021B/185

SEP 2 2 2022